HAL•LEONARD INSTRUMENTAL PLAY-ALONG

AUDIO
ACCESS
INCLUDED

PLAYBACK+
Speed • Pitch • Balance • Loop

TRUMPET
TOP HITS

Audio arrangements by Peter Deneff

To access audio visit:
www.halleonard.com/mylibrary

Enter Code
4061-9047-0284-7762

ISBN 978-1-4950-6576-7

7777 W. BLUEMOUND RD. P.O. BOX 13819 MILWAUKEE, WI 53213

Visit Hal Leonard Online at
www.halleonard.com

ADVENTURE OF A LIFETIME

TRUMPET

Words and Music by GUY BERRYMAN,
JON BUCKLAND, CHRIS MARTIN,
WILL CHAMPION, MIKKEL ERIKSEN
and TOR HERMANSEN

BUDAPEST

TRUMPET

Words and Music by GEORGE BARNETT
and JOEL POTT

To Coda ⊕

D.S. al Coda
(no repeat)

CODA
⊕

DIE A HAPPY MAN

TRUMPET

Words and Music by THOMAS RHETT,
JOE SPARGUR and SEAN DOUGLAS

EX'S & OH'S

TRUMPET

Words and Music by TANNER SCHNEIDER
and DAVE BASSETT

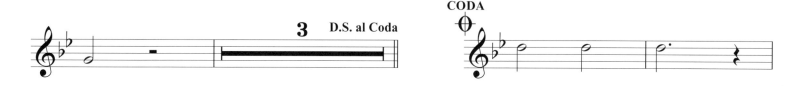

FIGHT SONG

TRUMPET

Words and Music by RACHEL PLATTEN
and DAVE BASSETT

HELLO

TRUMPET

Words and Music by ADELE ADKINS
and GREG KURSTIN

To Coda ⊕   **D.S. al Coda**

mp

CODA ⊕

1.

2.

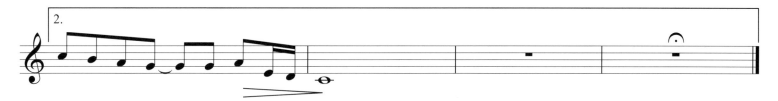

LET IT GO

TRUMPET

Words and Music by JAMES BAY
and PAUL BARRY

15

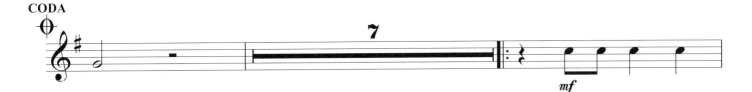

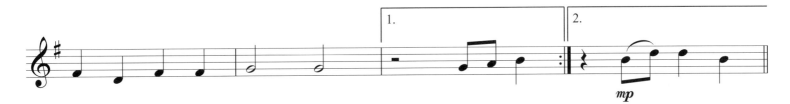

LOVE YOURSELF

TRUMPET

Words and Music by JUSTIN BIEBER,
BENJAMIN LEVIN and ED SHEERAN

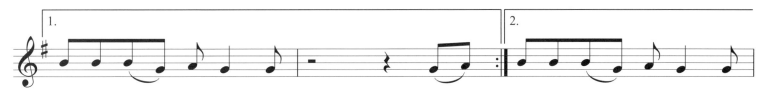

ONE CALL AWAY

TRUMPET

Words and Music by CHARLIE PUTH,
BREYAN ISAAC, MATT PRIME,
JUSTIN FRANKS, BLAKE ANTHONY CARTER
and MAUREEN McDONALD

PILLOWTALK

TRUMPET

Words and Music by LEVI LENNOX,
ANTHONY HANNIDES, MICHAEL HANNIDES,
ZAYN MALIK and JOE GARRETT

STITCHES

TRUMPET

Words and Music by TEDDY GEIGER,
DANNY PARKER and DANIEL KYRIAKIDES

WRITING'S ON THE WALL

from the film SPECTRE

TRUMPET

Words and Music by SAM SMITH
and JAMES NAPIER